Every Last Little Thing

AF624534

Liz Terrell

BookLeaf Publishing

Presentation by *BookLeaf Publishing*

Web: www.bookleafpub.com

E-mail: info@bookleafpub.com

ISBN: 9789357440141

First edition 2023

DEDICATION

To anyone who ever reads this.

You can do it.

You have enough.

You are enough.

ACKNOWLEDGEMENT

The only person who really knew that I was doing this was my partner Chris.

Thank you for your love, encouragement and support.

PREFACE

This book began as a new year challenge to myself. For one, I simply wanted to prove that I could do it. And two, I was looking for a catalyst to help renew my vigor and discipline to daily practice creativity. I have always had a fondness for writing- I keep a journal and consistently have a shelf full of blank ones close by waiting to be filled. I've accumulated an abundant collection of notes with lyrics to songs and words to poems and stories. Writing has been and will continue to be an invaluable tool for sifting through the tornado of thoughts that often trails through my mind.

I trust that you will find something within these pages that makes you think, makes you feel and helps you to know that you're not alone.

Big Ears

“She's got big ears”
All the better to hear you with my dear
Ears that hear as well as eyes that see
20/20

Listening, listening
As important as breathing
Into the music
and into the swing

Listening, listening
For Sarah's release and Ella's ease
and the space that the music leaves
in between

That pendulum feeling
swings silence to song
Did you hear it this time?
Could you play along?

Again, and again
‘til the cardrums fatigue
Try again tomorrow
with a bit more humility

Oh look!
Your ears are growing.

Every Last Little Thing

Be a lady
A pillar
A rock
A thrill

A kitten
A bitch
A wreck
Be still

Be a vision
A damsel
A storm
A light

A dream
A nightmare
Be wrong
Be right

Be Her
A Queen
A servant
A saint

A priestess
A gypsy
Be holy
And chaste

Be every
last
little
thing
except
a woman.

Bass Man

Bass Man
Masculine hands
Bend wood and metal
Fearless, Unrelenting
Completely in
and out
of control
His coax and caress
Moves her sound to surrender
She relents to their dance
Yielding to his hands
A musical trance
Between bass and man

It was Him

NO!
My internal conversation escaped into the morning sky.
I felt my heart skip a beat in my chest.
That familiar whisper in my head caused it to race with anticipation
of what it would hear next.

No.
I whispered more discreetly to myself.
How can I speak to the vastness of the sky
when I've not seen its beginning nor its end?
How dare I explain the depths of the sea
when my feet have never dared leave the shore?!
Did you REALLY just ask me to sing of Your love, grace, and mercy
when all I have known is the fight set against them?

Yet

My heart beats strong within me, and creates a longing for Him.

Where does my heart live?

Where did it learn to dream?
Can it not see what my eyes have seen and my ears have heard?

Impossibility is the place that we live.

Yet it still beats and grows inside of me as if it's trying to get out and fly.
How cruel would I be to give it wings? It could be shot down from the sky.
It could fall to the depths past the oceans shore to a place it has never been before!
Fear MUST dwell in the sky and the depths, for why else are they so unexplored?

But what if it knows something I don't know?
What if it can see another world?

Should I let my heart go
Then how would I know
How far it would travel
From the only life I've ever known.
Filled with such peace, and such quiet,
Such stillness and absolute lack of excitement.

Content, I sit with my nose in a book
Letting my eyes and ears do all the work
Only reading what others have seen and heard

Of a man's sacrifice and love I have learned...
was for me?

My mind took off running in search of such
rumors
It found many people willing to humor me

Week after week I sit and I watch
Looking for Him in every song
Searching each word spoken loud and clear
Yet never leaving truth ringing in my ears

My heart continues to beat with passion
although my soul is failing and losing hope
Wishing I could take back every inch of
exploration
I allowed it to seek in what would appear to be
Just another fairy tale

Maybe I should search in other places?
Look past the voices and into the faces
Of so many men and women who gather
together on a weekly basis

But I can see through their smiles
to the strings tightly holding their masks
That twinkle in their eyes is just a disguise for
the heart beating fast in THEIR chest
Seeking and wishing and some even praying

There is another world outside this one of
hopelessness

Does NO ONE have answers?
Is it all just a book of stories?
Why do we worship so ardently?
WHAT exactly ARE we worshipping?

Still my heart never waivers.
It wakes me every morning full of promise and
whispers of hope
A new day means new adventures
To find the answers I've yet to uncover of the
vastness of this man I call Lord

My heart must hear His voice again. Calling,
and calling, and calling.
It's the voice that my ears cannot dare to hear
when so clouded by this world's noise

That must be why it keeps beating and dreaming
and racing
and trying to burst from the home I've been
waiting
my whole life to leave.
Although it feels hopeless
This world offers safety, so I can never seem to
walk away completely.

I’m done with searching in fruitless places.
My heart has grown so loud it aches.
I pray that its beat is the alarm that He’s needed
to find me in my restless state.
My soul and my mind so full of fatigue
My body collapses in protest
I finally surrender and let myself just lay down
here to rest

A deep breath and exhale once my head hit the
floor
Suddenly my ears awakened to something I’d
never listened for.
Drumming and thumping the ground beneath
me. A single pair of feet.
Running and racing as fast as my heart, they
both shared the same beat.

Closer and closer they were gaining on me as I
laid there quiet and still.
Tears running down my face so afraid to hope
that what followed me
would be the answers that I would need to see
all my dreams fulfilled.

My heart was so close to escape, with nothing
left to hold it back
It beat faster and faster in pace with the feet that
followed so close in my tracks.

With my eyes closed tight my ears were in tune
with everything swirling around me
I could now hear his breath panting and
desperate knowing how close he was to finding
me.

I began to pray and repent
just knowing my life was at an end
For this MUST be fear catching up
With it close on my trail I began to recall
All the sin I'd committed since the moment that
began it all

That little girls heart breaking over and over
I could see where bitterness and anger set in,
Yet I could do nothing now but cry it all out after
years of holding it all in.
The beating continued on the ground so close it
was shaking the earth
This man knew he was gaining and closing in
toward the end of his pursuit.

I knew when he saw me for he stumbled and fell
But got up again just as quick,
I lay there waiting not even trying to hide
Ready to invite this fear inside
But instead he threw himself down beside me
Weeping tears of joy and relief

The beating drum of my heart stopped and burst forth
It was HIM!
The One I'd been looking for.
It was Him.
The One who followed me
It was Him
The whisper that made my heart beat
It was Him
Who was holding me, letting me weep
It was Him
The One who could set me free.
It was HIM.

The Lily

White as snow
it blooms
in the south of France
against the summer drenched
crimson skies of July
to the first brittle frost
of holy winter's night

See Her
petals delicate and strong
enduring and pure as a love song
She folds again 'til the time returns
to awaken from Her sleep.
Waiting to reveal the mysteries
of this divine fleur de lis.

Fog

Rain gently falls down the windows, nudging
me into a trance
I busy my hands with a methodical dance
Ice, measure, shake, pour
Turn the dial and music fills my soul

It wrenches my heart and I don't know why
Every day loving you is a complete surprise
The highest of highs and earth-shattering lows
Living in dissonance from note to note
Chet Baker on the record player
Bourbon in my glass
The smell of your cologne
I never stood a chance

You take the ground beneath me
I'm falling and floating in between
A trumpet calls from a distant fog
Suddenly I'm lost dancing in your arms
Your lips a trail of anticipation
I melt into your bed completely fixated
Lightning flashes across my eyes
The warmth of you meets the shock through my
spine

Body and soul tangle between us
Intertwining so intricately
You can't tell the difference

You're as familiar as home
and a completely new sensation
You're as stable as love
Unpredictable as fascination
Your gaze hypnotizes
I'm falling and grasping
Begging for that distant melody
to ground me back in reality

Ice clinks in my glass and steals me back
I gasp in unison with a record scratch
The fog of your memory
Fades like the scent of your cologne
I'm alone again
Silence rings in my ears
I remember you were never here
And I crumble into tears

Just Keep Talking

Feeling out of place
Like a child again
Stuck inside the world in my head
with not enough words to get out of it yet

Trying to make sense
looking for a space
That place made only for me
The one that I can fill
That I can fit
Only me
Just.
Me.

I need to find it.

Where do I go?
Where am I free?
Where am I comfortable?
Where am I me?

I take a deep breath
Trying to stay calm
I feel the water rising
Waiting to fill my lungs

How do I make the water go down?
Someone PLEASE help me make the water go down!
Can't anyone see it?
Please look down
All around
Can't you see it?!

Alone.

A crowded room.
A shoulder to cry on.
A desolate night.
A never-ending goodbye.
Always alone.

Can you just talk to me?
Please keep talking.
Keep asking.
My thoughts are trying to find the way out.
I need your help.
Ask me.
Always ask me.
Help me filter the words in my heart through my mouth.

Eventually I'll say what I really mean.
What I really feel is in there somewhere between all the babbling

The talking makes me vulnerable.
The asking makes you safe.
Come to the table.
and keep talking to me.
Just keep talking.

I Am

Where has the fire gone?
Where is that burning adrenaline coursing through my veins?
Flaming my cheeks. Tingling my fingers.
Heightening my senses.
The catalyst for my determination
Where is that burning need?

I've removed myself from the equation.
I have avoided compromising situations.
If I keep my distance I won't give away my deepest secret

I care too much.

No games. No contests. No equations or situations.
If I never give it thought or speak its name
It will simply go away.

Oh, sweet naivety.

It has reared its head in different ways.
It has battled with my senses.

It has paraded itself in the light of day
By a different name

I am unassuming.
I am calm.
I am nonchalant.
I am supportive.
I am waiting.

Waiting to take the stage and elevate myself
away.
Waiting to laugh pretentiously guised by
humility.
Waiting to say I never thought I would see the
day.
Waiting to parade. Waiting to strut.
Waiting to peel away and show my stuff.

I am hiding. I am bubbling. I am stirring the pot.
I am watching. I am learning. I am plotting my
next move.
I am frustrated. I am fighting. I am dueling
personalities.
I am ready to pounce. I am prepared to prove.

My primitive instincts are alive and thriving
fighting with the one within me that's still
striving
for peace

Is there no way to coexist?
Is there no chance for contentment?
Is this a countdown for when the poison will
win?
Won't peace numb my instinct to survive?
Will I blind my eyes with only the prize in sight?
Willing to die.
Will I only be satisfied when I'm trying to win?
Again and again and again and again

I am competition.

A Walk Through the Forest

A walk through the forest
Our cabin ahead
Wood for the fire
The leaves gleaming red

Wind through my skirt
Soft light through the trees
The smell of pine
Carried on the breeze

Cast iron porridge
A gentle flame
Family begins stirring
To start the day

A full wooden table
Sizzling eggs and bacon
Filling the room with
Laughing conversation

Imminent chores
Call us all to our day
Plowing and mending
and gardens to lay

The heat of noon
Drips saltily down
On burgeoning leaves
Where buds start to crown

The work is hard
Days tend to drone
But it's work worth doing
Building a home

Buckets refreshed
with cool river water
Shouldered back home
through forest and fodder

Sun sets in the west
The flaming hearth roars
Savory aromas permeate
Feet trample the door

I look around and wonder
How much better could this be?
Laughter and love
The warmth of family

A beautiful, simple life
So wild, so free
When did I ever get ...
An alarm clock rings.

X Marks the Spot

I am an artist.
Always have been and always will be.
Everything I will ever create is woven into me
hidden deep in the spider web of my DNA.

It is not the spirit of creation that an artist needs
But a heart strong enough
for the endless journey that awaits them
Full of ceaseless exploration and eternal
excavation.

My pilgrimage started ages ago
And I've been lost at sea ever since
If anything, I have more questions
Like where was the map in the midst of all this?!

Emotional flagellation lead me to a life of piracy
My specialty was map stealing
Comparison my analogy
For depth, strength, and transparency

Turning over stones as I turned over vinyl.
Magnifying the pedestals of lofty idols
Certain they hid secrets in between their
melodies.
Wasting my creative energy.

Tirelessly drawing up a treasure map
that will inevitably lead back
to ME

X marks the spot.

Sea Witch

This voice I use every day
often feels foreign to me
Like an entity that simply
resonates with noise
As though I have no claim
to its own patented use
It feels pillaged and pirated
Misshapen
and out of place
Every word leaves a trace
of bittersweet.
I'm beginning to believe
That a sea witch came
Enchanted me
And I sang my voice away

Lorelai

Life is a long adventure
Once you've had the pleasure of meeting her
Recklessly riled this feral and wild
Enchantress casts spells with her eyes
Loves like a firework, bright as the sunrise
Always a surprise
Intoxicating fascination for the rest of your life

Babble

We all begin as babes
turning noises into babble
and babble into chatter
and chatter into words
Words become phrases
We attempt to use
to be seen, heeded, and heard

Ideas bloom in our
malleable minds
What this? and that?
Hear me cry!
Why here? and there?
Echoes everywhere
Wails and cries
Whispers and sighs
Mouthing and talking
Shouting and calling

When did this noise become a voice?
And when did it become mine?

Where You Were Mine

It was never time for us.
Our orbits kept us at a distance.
Still we made a life and built
A home for our illusions.

You dressed me in your rhythm
Disarmed me with a glance
I answered your creation
With my own song and dance

You drew a smile from my lips
With our call and response
The movement in my hips
Strung you helplessly along

We forged our own little world
A utopian "Once upon a time"
We lived in the music we made
I was yours and you were mine

Morning, Noon and Night

Morning is for coffee
sleepy smiles and soft light
Slippers shuffling, neck kisses
Hot showers and bike rides
Slow and steady, ready for work
buttered toast, toothpaste
deep breathing, quiet music
Splashing water on your face

Noon is peaceful some days
Busy all the rest
Unpredictable and steady
as a weather man's forecast
Shoulder stretches, brisk walks
Ticking clocks, water breaks
To-do lists, meditation
Sugar rush to stay awake

Night comes with savory smells
Hot dinners and sipping red or white
Soapy dishes, Tv shows
Reading books and candlelight
Bath bombs, lavender
Evening's skin routine
Warm blanket, soft pillow
Another day, another dream

The Countdown

Like clock work
My heart begins the countdown
Although it's still hours away
Excitement? Adrenaline?
Beads of sweat get in the way
Painting makeup, deep breathing
Lip trills fill the room
like glitter from a costume

Blaze the trail I know so well
Load in through the back, traffic was hell
Full beat and a hoodie for sound check
Slippers on my feet
Hot tea, timidity
Trying to concentrate
Clear the stage, no more time to wait
Lock the door, keep the clock nearby
The countdown continues, rushing by

An inhale and she's in
Eyes locked in the mirror
Dressed up and zipped
A tuck and a touch
Scrutinizing until you can see her

Red lips emerge
Hips soft and round
Chin up, head high
It's the final countdown

Close your eyes, tune into your heart
Will it to slow down.
Take control of the throne.
This is your kingdom now.
Ten, Nine, Eight
Black out
Seven, Six, Five
The crowd
Four, Three, Two
Lights up.
One.

You've just begun.

Bridges

An endless plain of possibility
I survey my temptations
My choice today lasts infinitely
A test of character and patience

Desire draws me forward
A yearning moth to a flame
One step, a door swings open
Whispering my name

Winds of seduction
Coo gently from behind
Ushering me across
The bridges in my mind

Footsteps fracture stone
Left to crumble as I cross
I know exactly where this leads
But I think I'll pretend I'm lost

Thick air dissipates
at the point of no return
A desperate pant of passion
Sweet oxygen to burn

Reckless joy permeates
Every fiber of my being
A path falls clear before me
I surrender to its leading

Never again have I known
the temptation to look back
I burned my bridges on that day
Their ashes adorn my past

Aphrodisiac

Our night was hungry
Filled with naked decadence
A buffet of need

Hands and feet tangle
Moon beams set the table with
A bed sheet of silk

Only our breathing
To drink in between exhales
Kisses sip sweetly

Starved lips moved mountains
Climbing desire's summit
Continuously

Our night was hungry
We ate to our heart's content
Full, Satiated

Wild Flowers

Lizzie was a Rose
Determined and strong
She came in many colors
One for each of her songs
She bloomed with dreams
Integrity adorned her side
She was relentless and steady
As the rising tide

Sarah was an Iris
Full of courage and wisdom
Her grin danced with mischief
Like lights through a prism
She bloomed with hope
Summer, winter, spring, and fall
Sturdy and settled
The anchor of them all

Hannah was a Sunflower
All loyalty and adoration
Life was simply lovely
Everywhere a new sensation
She bloomed with curiosity
and grew taller every day
Knowing the strength of her roots
Would hold and never sway

Rebekah was a Daisy
Sensitive and pure
Fair as an aurora
Both unruly and demure
She bloomed with grace
As noble as a queen
Every year she became
More gentle and serene

Rose, Iris
Sunflower and Daisy
Grew deeply and wild and free
And though life would sway
through seasons of change
Together they made
the most beautiful bouquet.

www.ingramcontent.com/pod-product-compliance
Lightning Source LLC
Chambersburg PA
CBHW051744130826
49812CB00033B/991
* 9 7 8 9 3 5 7 4 4 0 1 4 1 *